THE ATLANTA FALCONS

BY THOMAS K. ADAMSON

EPIC

BELLWETHER MEDIA ★ MINNEAPOLIS, MN

EPIC

EPIC BOOKS are no ordinary books. They burst with intense action, high-speed heroics, and shadows of the unknown. Are you ready for an Epic adventure?

This edition first published in 2024 by Bellwether Media, Inc.

Library of Congress Cataloging-in-Publication Data

Names: Adamson, Thomas K., 1970- author.
Title: The Atlanta Falcons / by Thomas K. Adamson.
Description: Minneapolis, MN : Bellwether Media, 2024. | Series: Epic. NFL team profiles | Includes bibliographical references and index. | Audience: Ages 7-12 | Audience: Grades 2-3 | Summary: "Engaging images accompany information about the Atlanta Falcons. The combination of high-interest subject matter and light text is intended for students in grades 2 through 7"--Provided by publisher.
Identifiers: LCCN 2023021297 (print) | LCCN 2023021298 (ebook) | ISBN 9798886874679 (library binding) | ISBN 9798886876550 (ebook)
Subjects: LCSH: Atlanta Falcons (Football team)--History--Juvenile literature.
Classification: LCC GV956.A85 A33 2024 (print) | LCC GV956.A85 (ebook) | DDC 796.332/6409758231--dc23/eng/20230508
LC record available at https://lccn.loc.gov/2023021297
LC ebook record available at https://lccn.loc.gov/2023021298

Editor: Elizabeth Neuenfeldt   Designer: Gabriel Hilger

Printed in the United States of America, North Mankato, MN.

TABLE OF CONTENTS

SUPER PLAYOFF WIN

MATT RYAN

Falcons **quarterback** Matt Ryan drops back to pass. He runs and fakes a throw. He slides into the **end zone**. He scores a **touchdown**!

The Falcons surprise the Packers with a 44–21 win. They move on to **Super Bowl** 51!

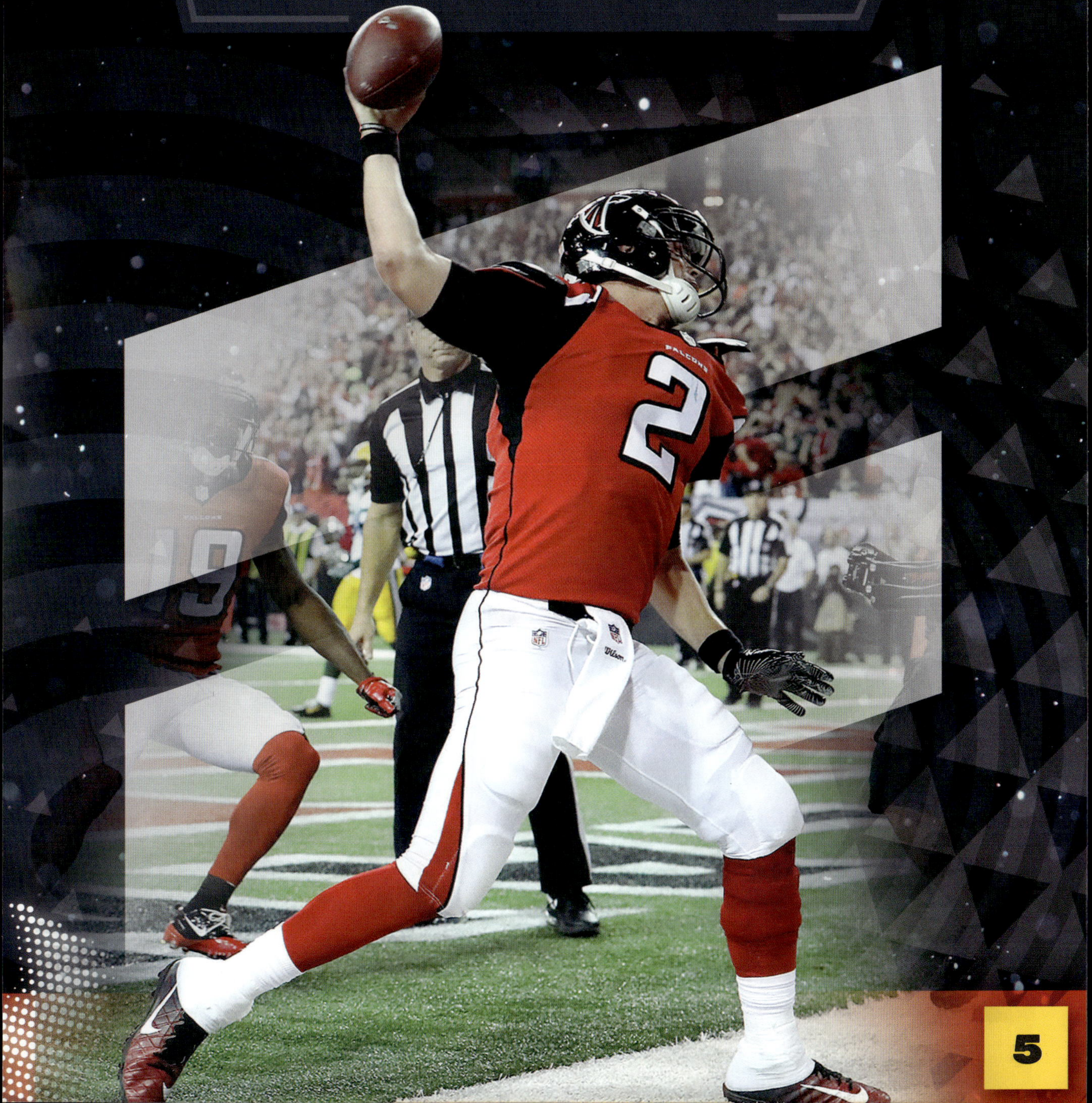

THE HISTORY OF THE FALCONS

In the 1960s, the National Football League (NFL) chose to start a new team in Atlanta, Georgia.

Rankin Smith paid $8.5 million for the **franchise**. The Falcons began play in the 1966 season.

1966 ATLANTA FALCONS

FIRST WIN

The Falcons' first win was against the New York Giants on November 20, 1966.

The new team started slow. Its first winning season was not until 1971.

A PROUD BIRD

A teacher won a contest to name the new team. Julia Elliott suggested Falcons. She said the bird has "great courage and fight."

STEVE BARTKOWSKI

The Falcons then **drafted** quarterback Steve Bartkowski. He led the team to its first **playoff** win in 1978.

Falcons fans suffered many losing seasons in the 1980s and 1990s.

1986 FALCONS GAME

But in 1998 the team finished with a 14–2 record. **Running back** Jamal Anderson had a big year. He helped the team reach Super Bowl 33. But they lost.

THE FALCONS AT SUPER BOWL 33

The Falcons struggled for much of the 2000s. They only reached the playoffs three times.

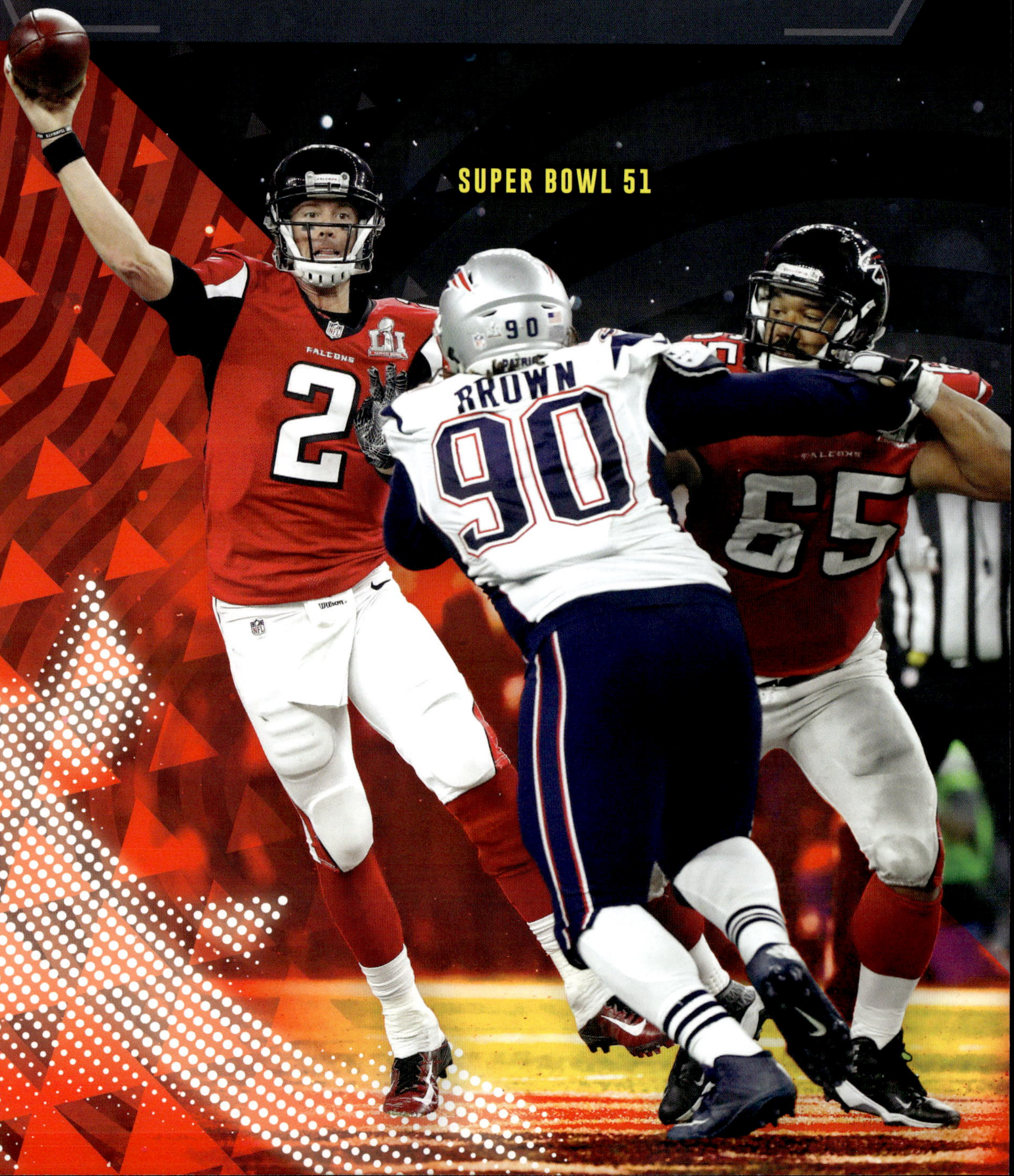

SUPER BOWL 51

Matt Ryan joined the team in 2008. He helped the Falcons. In 2017, he led the team to Super Bowl 51! But they lost.

THE FALCONS TODAY

FALCONS VS. SAINTS

The Falcons play their home games in Atlanta, Georgia. Mercedes-Benz **Stadium** was completed in 2017.

The team is part of the NFC South **division**. Their biggest **rival** is the New Orleans Saints.

LOCATION

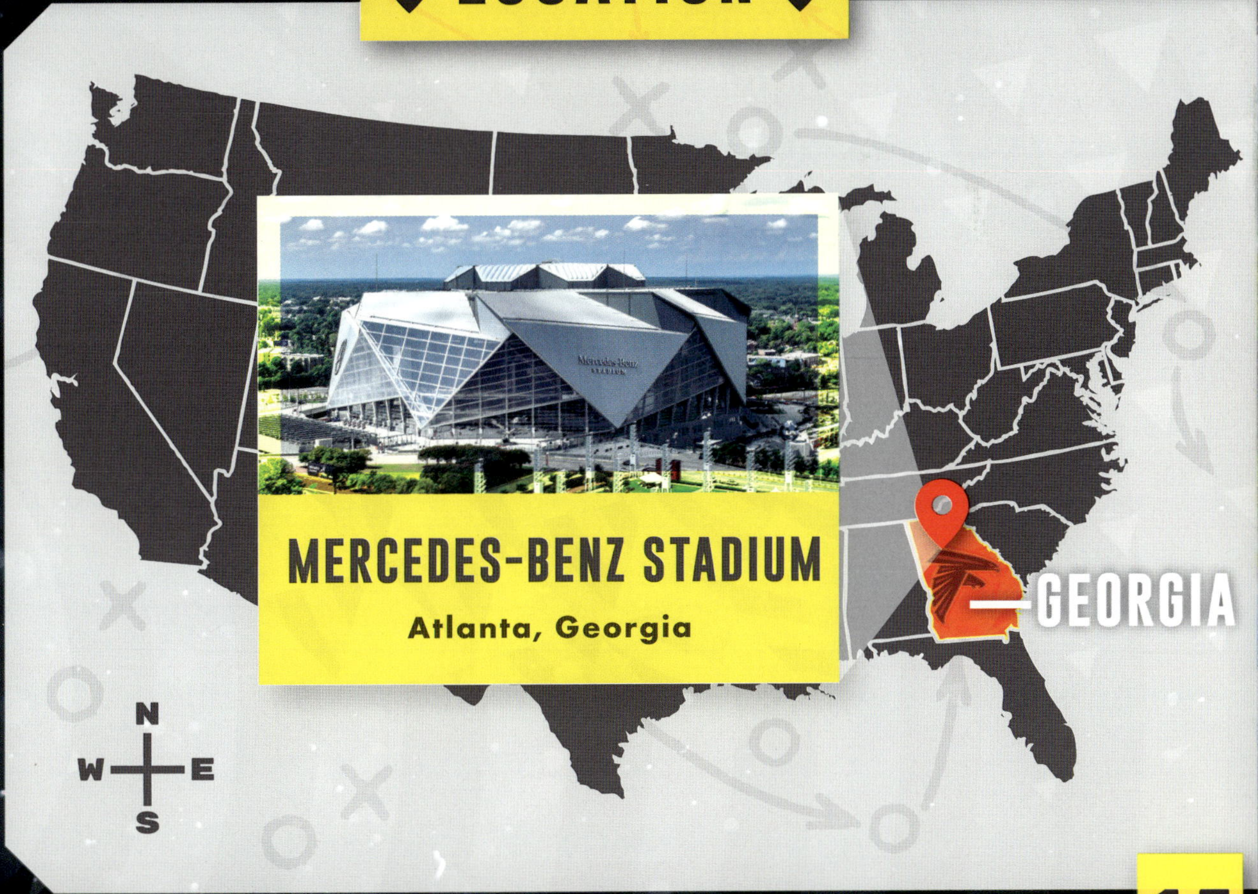

GAME DAY!

The Falcons' home stadium is a sea of red and black on game days. Fans love wearing the team's bold colors.

Atlanta was formed at the end of a railroad line. A train horn sounds when the Falcons score!

HIGH-TECH ROOF

Mercedes-Benz Stadium has a clear roof. It opens and closes in less than 10 minutes!

The Dirty Bird dance is a popular **tradition**. Jamal Anderson started this touchdown dance in the 1998 season. He turned his elbows out and flapped his arms like wings.

The dance still represents pride for Falcons fans!

DIRTY BIRD DANCE

★ FAMOUS PLAYERS ★

JEFF VAN NOTE

Center

Played 1969–1986

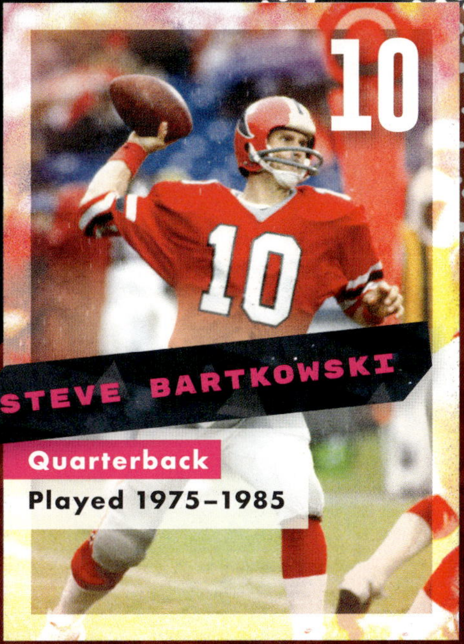

STEVE BARTKOWSKI

Quarterback

Played 1975–1985

WILLIAM ANDREWS

Running Back

Played 1979–1986

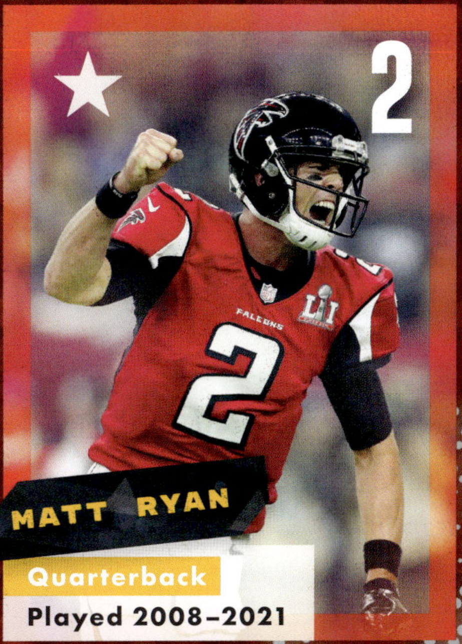

MATT RYAN

Quarterback

Played 2008–2021

JULIO JONES

Wide Receiver

Played 2011–2020

ATLANTA FALCONS FACTS

LOGO

JOINED THE NFL | 1966

NICKNAME | Dirty Birds

MASCOT

FREDDIE FALCON

CONFERENCE

National Football Conference (NFC)

COLORS

DIVISION | NFC South

Carolina Panthers

New Orleans Saints

Tampa Bay Buccaneers

STADIUM

MERCEDES-BENZ STADIUM

opened August 26, 2017

holds 71,000

TIMELINE

1965
Rankin Smith buys the Falcons franchise

1978
The Falcons win their first playoff game

1999
The Falcons play in Super Bowl 33

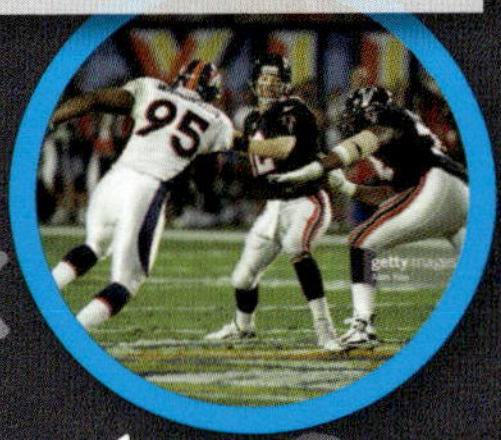

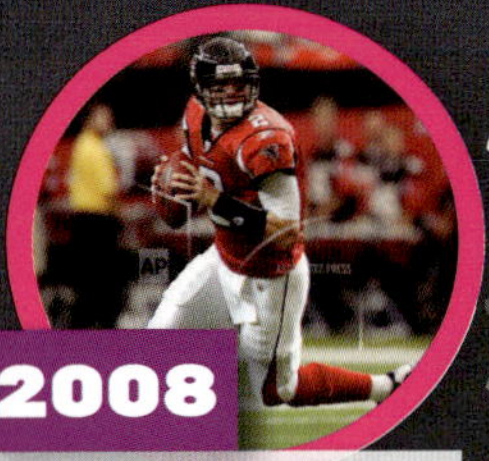

2008
Matt Ryan joins the team

2017
The Falcons play in Super Bowl 51

★ RECORDS ★

All-Time Passing Leader

Matt Ryan
59,735 yards

All-Time Rushing Leader

Gerald Riggs
6,631 yards

All-Time Receiving Leader

Julio Jones
12,896 yards

All-Time Scoring Leader

Matt Bryant
1,163 points

GLOSSARY

division—a group of NFL teams from the same area that often play against each other; there are eight divisions in the NFL.

drafted—chose a college athlete to play for a professional team

end zone—an area at either end of a football field; teams score points when they go into the end zone.

franchise—a team that is part of a league

playoff—a game played after the regular season is over; playoff games determine which teams play in the championship game.

quarterback—a player whose main job is to throw and hand off the ball

rival—a long-standing opponent

running back—a player whose main job is to run with the ball

stadium—an arena where sports are played

Super Bowl—the annual championship game of the NFL

touchdown—a score that occurs when a team crosses into their opponent's end zone with the football; a touchdown is worth six points.

tradition—a special way people celebrate or honor something

TO LEARN MORE

AT THE LIBRARY

Abdo, Kenny. *Atlanta Falcons.* Minneapolis, Minn.: Abdo Zoom, 2022.

Fishman, Jon M. *Matt Ryan.* Minneapolis, Minn.: Lerner Publications, 2018.

Whiting, Jim. *The Story of the Atlanta Falcons.* Mankato, Minn.: Creative Education, 2020.

ON THE WEB

FACTSURFER

Factsurfer.com gives you a safe, fun way to find more information.

1. Go to www.factsurfer.com.
2. Enter "Atlanta Falcons" into the search box and click 🔍.
3. Select your book cover to see a list of related content.

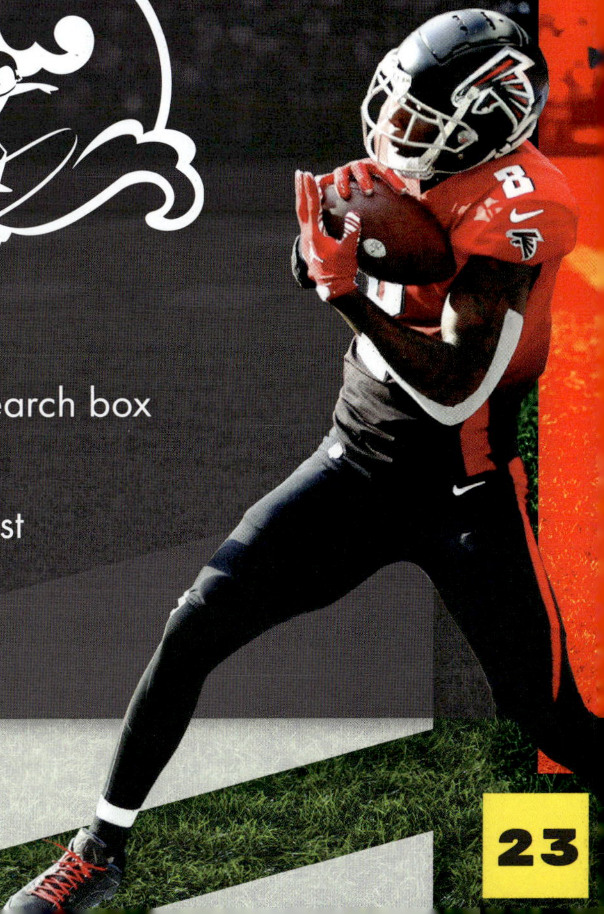

INDEX

The images in this book are reproduced through the courtesy of: Danny Karnik/ AP Images, cover (hero); alisafarov, cover (stadium); Paul Abel/ AP Images, p. 3; Ryan Kang/ AP Images, pp. 4, 8-9; Tribune Content Agency LLC/ Alamy, p. 5; Bob Verlin/ Contributor/ Getty, p. 6; Kevin Ruck, pp. 6-7; Focus On Sport/ Contributor/ Getty, pp. 9, 19 (Steve Bartowski, William Andrews); David Madison/ Contributor/ Getty, p. 10; Paul Spinelli/ NFL Photos/ AP Images, pp. 10-11; Greg Trott/ AP Images, p. 12; ZUMA Press Inc./ Alamy, p. 14; Nate Hovee, p. 15 (Mercedes-Benz Stadium); NFL/ Wikipedia, pp. 15 (Atlanta Falcons logo), 19 (Atlanta Falcons logo, Carolina Panthers logo, New Orleans Saints logo, Tampa Bay Buccaneers logo, NFC logo); Icon Sportswire/ Contributor/ Getty, p. 16; Peter Read Miller/ AP Images, pp. 16-17; AP Images, pp. 18 (inset), 21 (1965); Scott Cunningham/ Stringer/ Getty, pp. 18-19, 21 (Matt Bryant); All Messerschmidt Archive/ AP Images, p. 19 (Jeff Van Note); Tom Pennington/ Staff/ Getty Images, p. 19 (Matt Ryan); Rob Carr/ Staff/ Getty, p. 19 (Julio Jones); Scott Boehm/ AP Images, p. 20 (mascot); EQRoy, p. 20 (stadium); Bud Skinner/ AP Images, p. 21 (1978); Allen Kee/ Contributor/ Getty, p. 21 (1999); Dave Martin/ AP Images, p. 21 (2008); Kevin Terrell/ AP Images, p. 21 (2017); Joe Robbins/ AP Images, p. 21 (Matt Ryan); Gregory Trott/ AP Images, p. 21 (Gerald Riggs); Jamie Squire/ Staff/ Getty, p. 21 (Julio Jones); Action Plus Sports Images/ Alamy, p. 23.